GEMINI

HOROSCOPE

& ASTROLOGY

2025

Mystic Cat

Suite 41906, 3/2237 Gold Coast HWY

Mermaid Beach, Queensland, 4218

Australia

islandauthor@hotmail.com

Copyright © 2023 by Mystic Cat

Time set to Coordinated Universal Time Zone (UT±0)

Contents

Hello there, let me explain why my horoscope books may give different readings for each zodiac sign. The sky is always bustling with astrological activity, and I want to focus on what's most important for each star sign.

Every zodiac sign is unique, and the planets up above affect them differently. When I create horoscopes, I pay extra attention to the most critical astrological events for a specific sign. Some days, there might be lots of stuff happening in the stars, but one thing stands out as the essential factor for a particular zodiac sign.

I also consider which planet rules a sign and its associated element. This in-depth consideration helps me tailor my interpretations to match a sign's characteristics.

Ultimately, my goal is to provide you with unique advice and insights that match the cosmic influences for your sign. By focusing on what makes each sign special, I hope to help you understand yourself better and navigate the energies around you. Embracing your sign's strengths and challenges is the key to making my horoscopes feel uniquely aligned for you.

Cosmic Blessings,

Sia Sands

GEMINI 2025
HOROSCOPE & ASTROLOGY

Four Weeks Per Month

Week 1 – Days 1 - 7

Week 2 – Days 8 - 14

Week 3 – Days 15 - 21

Week 4 – Days 22 – Month-end

GEMINI

Gemini Dates: May 21st to June 20th

Zodiac Symbol: Twins

Element: Air

Planet: Mercury

House: Third

Color: Yellow

Gemini is the third astrological sign in the zodiac, belonging to the Air element. People born under the Gemini sign are known for their curious, adaptable, and communicative nature. The symbol of Gemini, the twins, represents duality, versatility, and the exchange of ideas.

Gemini individuals are quick-thinking, have intellectual curiosity, and love social interaction. They naturally adapt to different situations and are often skilled at seeing both sides of an issue. Ruled by Mercury, the planet of communication and intellect, Geminis are excellent communicators and enjoy engaging in discussions and debates.

Gemini is in the Third House of the zodiac, associated with communication, learning, and short journeys. This placement highlights Gemini's inclination toward education, gathering information, and connecting with others through various means.

Yellow is often associated with Gemini due to its vibrancy, intellect, and connection to mental agility. This color reflects the active and versatile nature of Gemini individuals.

In summary, Gemini represents versatility, communication, and intellectual curiosity. Those born under this sign tend to be adaptable, social, and skilled at processing and sharing information. Their ability to see different perspectives and engage in meaningful conversations makes them excellent communicators and collaborators.

The Chinese Zodiac is a system that assigns an animal sign to each year in a 12-year cycle, and each animal is associated with certain personality traits and characteristics.

The Year of the Snake, in particular, holds special significance within Chinese culture and is rich in symbolism.

2025

The Chinese Year of the Snake

Geminis are known for their curiosity, adaptability, and quick-witted nature. They possess a dualistic personality that allows them to explore various perspectives and ideas. When the Year of the Snake arrives, it introduces an intriguing blend of energies that can engage and stimulate the Gemini mind.

During this year, Geminis might find themselves drawn to the Snake's symbolism of communication and intuition. The Snake is known for its ability to communicate verbally and nonverbally, which resonates well with Gemini's gift for practical expression.

The Year of the Snake encourages Geminis to dive deeper into their natural curiosity. It's a time for exploration and intellectual growth, where Geminis can satisfy their thirst for knowledge by delving into intriguing subjects. Just as snakes are adept at sensing their surroundings, Geminis might develop a heightened awareness of the subtleties in their environment.

Geminis' adaptability could synergize with the Snake's ability to navigate various terrains. This year might present opportunities for Geminis to adapt their communication style to different situations and audiences, enhancing their ability to connect with others.

In relationships, the Year of the Snake could inspire Geminis to develop a deeper understanding of emotional nuances. Geminis might find themselves tuning in to others' emotions and forming connections based on empathy and compassion.

While Geminis are known for their quick thinking, the Year of the Snake invites them to embrace a more reflective approach. It doesn't mean sacrificing their nimble minds; instead, it's about combining their agility with thoughtful consideration of their actions and decisions.

Ultimately, the Year of the Snake allows Geminis to expand their mental horizons, refine their communication skills, and connect more profoundly with others. By embracing the Snake's qualities of perception and expression, Geminis can make the most of this year's energy to enrich their minds and relationships.

GEMINI 2025
HOROSCOPE & ASTROLOGY

Moon Ingress Capricorn: When the Moon moves into Capricorn, it's like donning your sharpest business suit and setting your sights on the peaks of success. Capricorn's energy is all about ambition, discipline, and unyielding determination to climb higher. Your emotions feel more serious and focused, and you'll likely be driven to tackle your goals with renewed vigor.

New Moon: Brace yourselves, stargazers, because the New Moon is like a cosmic clean slate, an enchanted moment to manifest your dreams. This lunar phase brings fresh beginnings, and in Capricorn's territory, it's all about your career and public image. The universe is ready to assist, so take a deep breath, set your goals, and let it work magic. It's your time to shine.

Moon Ingress Aquarius: As the Moon saunters into Aquarius, it's like a breath of fresh air for your soul. Aquarius' energy is rebellious, innovative, and all about celebrating individuality. You feel the urge to break free from the ordinary, embrace your quirks, and connect with your tribe. Your social consciousness ignites, and you're ready to revolutionize the world.

JANUARY WEEK ONE

Brace yourself for a celestial dance of romance and dreaminess as Venus elegantly glides into Pisces. This cosmic waltz infuses your love life and personal style with an aura of enchantment.

Get ready to fasten your cosmic seat belts because a clash of titans unfolds as Mars opposes Pluto. This astral duel demands your utmost wisdom; channel this potent energy into an unwavering pursuit of your goals.

The ethereal serenity of Pisces envelopes your emotional landscape as the Moon gracefully enters this sign. Pisces' energy invites introspection and the surrender to the ebb and flow of emotions.

The heavens offer a celestial pat on the back as the Sun forms a harmonious sextile with Saturn. It's like a cosmic nod of approval for your unwavering dedication and tireless efforts. This planetary alignment brings stability and a palpable sense of achievement.

Brace yourself for a cosmic gearshift as the Moon boldly enters Aries. In the realm of the Ram, your passions ignite like a blazing comet.

As Mercury gracefully enters Capricorn, your thoughts take on a more practical and disciplined tone. It's like a cosmic executive taking charge of your mental space, encouraging structured thinking and goal-oriented communication.

With the Moon's playful entrance into Gemini, your emotions become as changeable as the wind. It's like a cosmic storyteller, urging you to explore ideas and connect with others through lively conversations. Your curiosity knows no bounds during this lunar phase.

The Moon's gentle transition into Cancer envelops you in a cocoon of emotional sensitivity. A warm, nurturing energy surrounds you, and the desire for comfort and familiarity becomes paramount. It encourages you to connect with your feelings and seek solace in familiar surroundings.

When Mars forms a harmonious trine with Neptune, it's a cosmic blend of passion and dreams. This aspect fuels your actions with creative and spiritual energy, allowing you to pursue your goals.

JANUARY WEEK TWO

As the Sun forms a harmonious trine with Uranus, expect a dash of cosmic innovation and excitement. It's like a celestial inventor, inspiring you to break free from routines and embrace new experiences. This aspect encourages you to express your individuality and explore uncharted territories.

The Full Moon, the climax of the lunar cycle, shines a spotlight on your emotions and culminations. It's a time of heightened feelings and realizations. Use this lunar phase to release what no longer serves you and celebrate your achievements.

With the Moon's grand entrance into Leo, your emotions have a theatrical flair. It's like a cosmic stage where you can express your inner performer with confidence and flair. It is a time to shine, seek recognition, and enjoy life's pleasures.

Venus Square Jupiter: When Venus squares off with Jupiter, it's a cosmic war between love and excess. This aspect can bring extravagance and indulgence into your relationships and finances.

🜂 When the Sun opposes Mars, cosmic forces clash in a fiery showdown. It's like a celestial tug-of-war between your desires and your actions. This aspect stirs up assertiveness and may lead to conflicts or power struggles. Harness this intense energy to fuel your ambitions, but remember to tread carefully, as impulsiveness can lead to heated situations.

🌙 The Moon's ingress into meticulous Virgo encourages a focus on detail and practicality. You'll find satisfaction in organizing and tidying up your physical space and thoughts. It's a great time for productivity and taking care of those small, nagging tasks.

🗡 The Sun's harmonious sextile with Neptune invites a touch of magic into your life. You'll find beauty in the subtle and mysterious.

💜 Venus's conjunction with Saturn brings a sense of responsibility and commitment to your relationships and pleasures. It's like a cosmic promise to take love and enjoyment seriously. This aspect encourages long-term commitments and stability in matters of the heart.

JANUARY WEEK THREE

As the Moon gracefully moves into Libra's harmonious realm, you'll seek balance and harmony in your interactions with others. This cosmic influence enhances your diplomacy and desire for fairness. It's an ideal time to mend fences and strengthen relationships.

Mercury's harmonious sextile with Saturn and Venus adds intellectual finesse to your communications. You'll find it easier to express your thoughts with clarity and charm. This cosmic trio enhances your ability to negotiate and make well-informed decisions.

The Sun's entrance into Aquarius ushers in a period of innovation and humanitarian focus. You'll be drawn to unconventional ideas and collective endeavors, like a cosmic inventor seeking to revolutionize the world.

When the Sun aligns with transformative Pluto, it's a powerhouse of change and rebirth. This aspect encourages you to dig deep and face your inner truths.

As the Moon moves into passionate Scorpio, this cosmic influence encourages you to explore the mysteries of life and transformation with open arms.

When Mars forms a harmonious sextile with Uranus, your energy gets a cosmic boost. It's like a rocket of motivation, propelling you into action with innovative and daring approaches. Embrace the spirit of adventure!

Mercury's trine with Uranus sparks mental brilliance and inventive thinking. Your mind is like a lightning storm of creative ideas. Embrace this time to brainstorm and explore new concepts.

As the Moon enters adventurous Sagittarius, your emotions seek freedom and exploration. You'll crave new experiences and the broader perspectives that come with them.

Venus forms a harmonious trine with Mars, igniting passion and harmony in your relationships. Enjoy the sparks of romance and creative collaboration.

Venus sextile Uranus brings excitement and spontaneity to your love life and personal style. Embrace your unique quirks and be open to unexpected romantic adventures.

JANUARY WEEK FOUR

As the Moon joins Mercury in Aquarius, your emotions align with your intellectual pursuits. You'll be drawn to like-minded individuals and social causes that resonate with your values.

Mercury's conjunction with Pluto ushers in a time of deep and transformative conversations. It's a cosmic dive into the mysteries of the mind and the power of words.

The New Moon signals a fresh start and a blank canvas for your intentions. Set your goals and aspirations for the lunar cycle ahead.

Uranus turns direct, infusing your life with innovation and unexpected changes. Embrace the shifts, as they bring opportunities for personal growth.

As the Moon glides into intuitive Pisces, your emotions become compassionate. It's a time to connect with your spiritual side and express empathy.

The Sun's trine with Jupiter brings optimism and expansion. Confidence soars and abundance abounds.

💜 When Venus cozies up to Neptune in the celestial ballroom, it's as if your heart is bathed in the soft glow of moonlight. Love and romance take on a dreamy, ethereal quality during this enchanting alignment.

As the Moon strides into fiery Aries, your emotions catch fire with passion and assertiveness. This cosmic shift ignites a surge of energy within you, making you feel invincible and ready to tackle new challenges head-on. The world becomes your playground, and you're eager to be the initiator of exciting adventures.

Mercury's harmonious trine with expansive Jupiter opens the floodgates of communication and intellectual exploration. Your mind becomes a fertile ground for big ideas, and your words flow with wisdom and optimism.

When the Moon finds its haven in sensual Taurus, your emotions settle into a serene and grounded state. You'll seek comfort in life's simple pleasures, whether savoring delicious cuisine, indulging in tactile luxuries, or enjoying the beauty of nature. This cosmic influence encourages you to build emotional security and stability.

🐾 Venus's entrance into fiery Aries infuses your love life and personal style with a burst of independent and adventurous energy. During this cosmic phase, you won't shy away from taking bold steps in matters of the heart. If you've been waiting for the perfect moment to make your move or express your affections, now is the time to do so with unwavering confidence.

⏩ With Jupiter resuming its direct motion, a cosmic green light is given to your dreams and ambitions. Projects and plans that may have been in a holding pattern can now progress with renewed momentum.

As the Moon transitions into inquisitive Gemini, your social butterfly wings unfurl. Your curiosity is piqued, and your communication skills shine. You'll relish engaging with diverse people and topics, making each interaction a delightful adventure.

💜 Venus's harmonious sextile with transformative Pluto adds depth to your relationships and desires. This passionate cosmic connection encourages you to explore profound depths as your affections take on a magnetic allure, drawing a journey of emotional transformation.

As the Moon gracefully takes residence in nurturing Cancer, your emotions find solace in the comforts of home and family. You'll prioritize the people and places that provide emotional security, and your intuitive faculties will be heightened during this lunar phase.

The Sun's conjunction with Mercury illuminates your thoughts and communications with clarity and insight. Your mind is sharp, and you can express your ideas with precision. It's an ideal time for intellectual pursuits and engaging in meaningful conversations.

Mars forms a harmonious trine with Saturn, infusing your actions with discipline and determination. This cosmic alignment empowers you to pursue your goals with a structured and patient approach, ensuring that your efforts yield long-lasting results.

Later, as the Moon moves into confident Leo, you'll exude self-assuredness and seek opportunities to shine in the spotlight. Your creativity and leadership abilities come to the forefront, making it an excellent time to showcase your talents.

The Sun squares off with Uranus, sparking unexpected twists and turns in your life. This aspect encourages you to embrace change and be open to innovative ideas, even if they disrupt your routine. Flexibility and adaptability are essential during this electrifying cosmic event.

The Full Moon shines a celestial spotlight on your emotions and relationships. It's a time of culmination and illumination, where you can celebrate achievements and gain insights into your closest connections.

The Moon's transition into meticulous Virgo brings attention to detail and a desire for order. You'll find satisfaction in focusing on practical tasks.

On Valentine's Day, Mercury gracefully glides into dreamy Pisces, infusing your thoughts and conversations with empathy and intuition. During this cosmic phase, you'll prioritize emotional connections and creative expression in your interactions with others. It's a time when poetry and compassion flow naturally in your communication style, making it an extraordinary period for romantic and heartfelt conversations.

As the Moon gracefully glides into charming Libra, your emotions find solace in pursuing harmony and equilibrium. You naturally seek fairness in your interactions and surroundings during this cosmic dance. In your relationships, you're more attuned to the needs of others, making it an ideal time to cultivate peace and understanding in your connections.

As the Moon delves deeper into the enigmatic waters of Scorpio, your emotions take on a more intense and reflective quality. It's as if a cosmic veil is lifted, revealing the hidden aspects of your innermost feelings. During this phase, you may experience heightened intuition and a desire to explore the profound mysteries of existence. Emotional authenticity becomes paramount as you navigate the depths of your soul and engage in meaningful, transformative experiences.

The Sun's transition into compassionate Pisces marks a period of heightened sensitivity and artistic inspiration. Pisces, the sign of dreams and imagination, invites you to dive into the sea of emotions and creativity.

FEBRUARY WEEK THREE

The Moon's move into adventurous Sagittarius infuses your emotions with optimism and a thirst for knowledge. Under this celestial influence, you're drawn to new experiences, philosophical insights, and the vast landscapes of the mind. It's as if your spirit yearns for freedom and expansion, urging you to explore the outer world and the realms of higher understanding. It is when you may feel compelled to embark on a physical or intellectual journey that broadens your horizons and aligns with your thirst for truth.

Mercury's square with expansive Jupiter creates a dynamic interplay between your thoughts and your quest for knowledge. While this aspect fosters enthusiasm and a hunger for learning, balancing visionary thinking and practicality is essential. Your ideas may be grand and far-reaching, but remaining grounded in reality is necessary to manifest your dreams effectively. Be mindful of overcommitting or making promises you might struggle to keep. This celestial conversation encourages you to combine your boundless optimism with a healthy dose of realism, creating a solid foundation for your visionary pursuits.

When the Moon gracefully enters the pragmatic realm of Capricorn, your emotions take on a more grounded and disciplined tone. This lunar phase encourages you to focus on your long-term goals and responsibilities. You'll find satisfaction in making practical plans and taking steps toward your ambitions. It's a time to cultivate resilience and a strong sense of purpose, allowing you to navigate challenges with determination.

Mars turning direct is like a cosmic ignition switch, bringing renewed energy and momentum to your endeavors. After reflection and reevaluation, you're ready to move forward with your plans and initiatives. The fiery energy of Mars propels you toward your goals, and obstacles that once stood in your way can be overcome with newfound vigor. It's a time to channel your passions and confidently assert your desires.

As the Moon transitions into innovative Aquarius, your emotions align with a sense of independence and a desire to break free from the ordinary. You'll be drawn to unconventional ideas. This lunar phase encourages you to embrace your uniqueness and foster a sense of community.

FEBRUARY WEEK FOUR

Mercury's conjunction with Saturn signifies a time of structured and disciplined thinking. Your mental faculties are sharp, and you approach your responsibilities with diligence. This aspect encourages careful planning and attention to detail, making it an excellent period for tackling complex tasks and organizing your thoughts. While your mind may feel grounded, it's also receptive to innovative ideas.

Mercury's sextile with Uranus adds an element of innovation to thinking and communication. Your mind is open to unconventional and progressive concepts. This aspect invites you to explore horizons and engage in stimulating conversations.

The New Moon represents a fresh start and a blank canvas for your intentions. It's a potent time to set new goals, initiate projects, and plant the seeds of your aspirations. During this lunar phase, take a moment to reflect on what you wish to manifest in your life and set clear intentions. The energy of the New Moon supports your efforts to create a brighter future filled with possibilities.

As the Moon boldly enters the fiery sign of Aries, your emotions ignite with a sense of spontaneity and assertiveness. You'll feel a surge of energy and a desire to take action. This lunar phase encourages you to follow your passions and enthusiastically tackle challenges.

Venus, the planet of love and beauty, turns retrograde, prompting reflection and reevaluation in matters of the heart and aesthetics. It's a time to revisit and reassess your relationships, values, and personal style. Past loves and connections may resurface, offering you the chance to heal and grow in matters of the heart.

Mercury's conjunction with dreamy Neptune blurs the lines between reality and imagination in your communications and thoughts. Your mind is open to creative and intuitive insights, making it a time for artistic expression and spiritual exploration. However, be mindful of potential misunderstandings or vague communication during this hazy transit.

The Sun's square with expansive Jupiter brings a sense of optimism and grandeur. Under this cosmic influence, balance aspirations with practicality.

MARCH WEEK ONE

Mercury's transition into assertive Aries marks a period of direct and bold communication. Your thoughts and words become more forthright and confident, and you'll feel a sense of urgency in your mental pursuits.

The Moon's move into sensual Taurus offers a moment of earthly indulgence and sensory pleasure. You'll find comfort in simple delights, from good food to a cozy atmosphere. Emotionally, stability and security become paramount, and you may seek to create a harmonious environment that nurtures your senses.

Mercury's sextile with transformative Pluto deepens your mental acuity and opens the door to robust conversations and profound insights. Your ability to dig beneath the surface and uncover hidden truths is heightened, and you may engage in deep and meaningful discussions.

As the Moon transitions into a versatile Gemini, your mind becomes agile and curious. You'll be drawn to various interests and social interactions, craving mental stimulation and diversity in your experiences.

A harmonious trine between the Sun and Mars brings energy and motivation to your life. Your actions align with your desires, making it an ideal time to pursue your goals with confidence and enthusiasm.

As the Moon gracefully enters Leo, your emotions take on a more dramatic and expressive flair. You'll seek recognition and attention, and there's a desire to shine and be the center of the spotlight. It's a cosmic invitation to embrace your creativity and indulge in activities that make your heart sing.

Mercury's conjunction with Venus combines the power of thought and love, making your conversations and connections particularly charming and harmonious. Your words are infused with grace and diplomacy, and you'll find it easy to express your affections and create beauty through language and expression.

The Moon's transition into Virgo encourages a more analytical and detail-oriented approach to your emotions. You may feel compelled to organize and improve your surroundings and care for practical matters.

MARCH WEEK TWO

The Sun's conjunction with Saturn marks a time of focused determination and commitment. You'll approach responsibilities with discipline and a strong sense of duty. This cosmic influence encourages you to make long-term plans and build a solid foundation.

The Full Moon shines a spotlight on your achievements and relationships. It's a time for both celebration and evaluation. Your emotions are heightened, and you'll gain clarity about your partnerships and personal goals. Use this lunar phase to release and make room for new opportunities.

The Sun's sextile with Uranus brings excitement and innovation to your life. You're open to change and may experience sudden insights or unexpected opportunities. Embrace your individuality and be open to exploring new horizons.

As the Moon continues its journey into balanced Libra, you'll seek harmony and fairness in your interactions. Your social and diplomatic skills are heightened, and you'll be inclined to seek compromise and create peaceful connections with others.

◎ Mercury's retrograde journey invites reflection and review in your communication and thought processes. It's as if the cosmic messenger takes a step back, urging you to revisit and reevaluate your ideas, conversations, and plans. During this time, be patient with potential disruptions and miscommunications, and use the retrograde energy to gain a fresh perspective on matters that require attention.

☽ As the Moon delves into the intense and transformative sign of Scorpio, your emotions take on a deep and probing quality. This lunar phase encourages you to explore the mysteries of your inner world and embrace your emotional intensity. It's when you may uncover hidden truths and experience profound transformations in your psyche.

☽ As the Moon transitions into the adventurous sign of Sagittarius, a spirit of optimism and curiosity washes over you. It's a cosmic invitation to explore new horizons, seek knowledge, and embark on exciting journeys of the mind or body.

MARCH WEEK THREE

When the Sun forms a conjunction with dreamy Neptune, your inner world becomes awash with inspiration and creativity. This celestial alignment encourages you to tap into your intuition, imagination, and spiritual depths. It's a time to embrace artistic and mystical pursuits, acts of compassion and empathy. Your dreams and visions hold a special significance during this phase.

The Sun's entrance into Aries heralds the Vernal Equinox, marking the beginning of spring and a new astrological year. The energy of Aries is bold, assertive, and pioneering, encouraging you to take initiative and initiate new projects. It's a time of fresh starts and a surge of vitality.

Venus' sextile with Pluto adds a touch of intensity and depth to your relationships and desires. This cosmic connection encourages you to explore the depths of your emotional connections and seek transformation in your partnerships. It's a potent time to understand your desires and forge powerful bonds.

☺ The Sun's conjunction with Mercury is akin to a burst of mental clarity and eloquence. Your thoughts are razor-sharp, and your words carry a compelling power. This alignment supports clear and efficient communication, making it an opportune moment to express your ideas and engage in meaningful dialogues.

◯ Mercury's sextile with Pluto encourages meaningful conversations. Your words can unveil hidden truths and set in motion transformative processes. It's a period when you explore subjects that pique your curiosity.

☽ As the Moon continues its celestial journey, moving into ethereal Pisces, your emotional sensitivity and intuition reach new heights. It's as if the universe beckons you to explore the world of dreams, creativity, and spiritual connection. Activities like art, meditation, and acts of kindness become a source of solace.

● With the Black Moon's entry into Scorpio, the depths of your emotions may stir. This cosmic event encourages introspection and a willingness to confront unresolved issues. It's an opportunity to embrace your shadow self and acknowledge those hidden aspects of your psyche.

MARCH WEEK FOUR

Venus's entrance into Pisces adds a layer of romance and idealism to your relationships. Your capacity for compassion and understanding deepens, fostering emotional connections and spiritual bonding. Acts of kindness and selflessness are particularly appealing, and you find beauty in the realms of love and empathy.

The conjunction of Venus and Neptune amplifies the dreamy and romantic atmosphere. This period is marked by heightened creativity and a longing to experience transcendent love and beauty—imagination soars, drawing you toward artistic and spiritual pursuits.

As the Moon enters the fiery sign of Aries, a surge of energy and assertiveness courses through you. It's a cosmic call to action, urging you to seize the reins and face challenges head-on. Confidence radiates from your every move as you embrace the thrill of taking the lead.

The New Moon marks a fresh beginning, a cosmic canvas on which to paint your aspirations. It's an opportunity to set new intentions and sow the seeds of your desires. The world is yours to shape, and this lunar phase symbolizes renewal and limitless potential.

As the Moon gracefully moves into versatile Gemini, your emotions take on a curious and adaptable quality. This lunar phase inspires mental agility and a thirst for knowledge. You enjoy stimulating conversations, learning new things, and exploring various interests.

Saturn's sextile with Uranus presents a unique cosmic alignment that harmonizes the old with the new. This aspect encourages innovation and progress within the framework of tradition and stability. It's as though you're building upon a strong foundation while adapting to the evolving demands of the future.

Mars' sextile with Uranus sets the stage for a burst of dynamic energy and a willingness to embrace change. During this period, you're inclined to take bold and unconventional actions, making it an ideal time for tackling challenges and breaking free from restrictions.

Mars' trine with Saturn creates a harmonious blend of discipline and ambition. This cosmic connection empowers you to pursue your goals with determination and patience. It's as though you have the stamina to overcome obstacles and build lasting achievements.

APRIL WEEK ONE

○ The Sun's sextile with Jupiter expands your horizons and amplifies your optimism. It's like a cosmic green light for pursuing your goals and dreams. This aspect brings good fortune and a sense of abundance, making it an opportune time to take risks and embrace new opportunities.

💜 Venus's trine with Mars enhances the harmony in your relationships and adds a touch of passion to your interactions. This cosmic connection fosters romantic and creative energies, making it a favorable period for expressing affection and pursuing artistic endeavors.

🖤 The conjunction of Venus and Saturn emphasizes commitment and responsibility in your relationships. During this time, you may seek stability and longevity in your partnerships. It's an ideal phase for making serious decisions about the future of your connections.

🔄 As Mercury turns direct, you'll feel a sense of clarity and forward momentum in your communications and decision-making. The challenges and delays of the retrograde period are behind you, allowing you to move ahead with confidence and a clear vision.

Venus's sextile with Uranus brings an exciting and electrifying energy to your relationships and creative endeavors. It's as if a cosmic spark has been ignited, infusing your interactions with a sense of novelty and spontaneity. During this period, you may be drawn to unconventional forms of expression and open to exciting, unexpected connections.

As the Moon gracefully enters meticulous Virgo, your emotions take on a practical and analytical tone. This lunar phase encourages attention to detail, and you may find satisfaction in tending to your daily tasks and responsibilities with precision and care. It's a time for organizing and refining your world.

Transitioning into Libra, the Moon brings a sense of balance and harmony to your emotional landscape. This lunar phase highlights your desire for connection and beauty, making it an ideal time for socializing and appreciating the aesthetics of life. Your interactions with others are graced with diplomacy and a desire for peace. It's a perfect time for fostering connections and finding beauty in the symphony of life.

The Full Moon, a powerful climax in the lunar cycle, illuminates the sky with its radiant energy. This period marks a culmination, a time to reap what you've sown in the preceding weeks. It's a moment for reflection and celebration as the intentions you set during the New Moon now come to fruition.

Venus turns direct, ending its retrograde journey. This celestial shift clarifies matters of the heart and your sense of beauty. You may find that your relationships and values become more straightforward to navigate. It's a time to resolve any lingering issues and move forward with a newfound understanding.

As the Moon moves into passionate Scorpio, your emotions delve deep into intensity and transformation. This lunar phase invites you to explore the hidden corners of your psyche, making it an ideal time for introspection and embracing your inner power. Your emotional experiences are profound and magnetic. It's a time when you may feel an urge to explore the mysteries of life and confront deep truths. Your emotional depth and intuition are heightened, leading you to explore uncharted emotional territory.

With Mercury's entrance into bold and fiery Aries, your communication style becomes assertive and direct. It's as if your words carry a spark of enthusiasm and courage. This placement fosters a pioneering spirit in your thoughts and ideas, making it an excellent time to start new projects or share your innovative concepts.

When Mercury aligns with dreamy Neptune, your mental landscape takes on a surreal and imaginative quality. It's like a cosmic poet's pen, allowing you to weave words and ideas into beautiful, ethereal tapestries. This aspect encourages creativity, intuition, and empathy in your communication. You may find yourself drawn to artistic or spiritual pursuits, using language to evoke emotions and inspire others.

Mars's ingress into Leo infuses your actions with passion and a desire for recognition. You're unapologetically assertive about pursuing your wishes and goals. This placement encourages you to take center stage and express your individuality with flair. Your creative energy surges, making it ideal to showcase your talents and pursue projects that ignite your passion.

When Mars forms a harmonious trine with Neptune, your actions align with your dreams and ideals. It enhances intuition, making it an excellent time for creative and humanitarian endeavors.

Easter Sunday symbolizes rebirth and renewal, symbolizing the emergence of light and hope. It's a time for reflection, forgiveness, and new beginnings.

This celestial connection adds excitement and unpredictability to your relationships and social life. This aspect encourages you to celebrate your individuality and explore unconventional forms of love.

When Mercury forms a sextile with transformative Pluto, your communication becomes profound and insightful. This aspect encourages deep and meaningful conversations that can lead to personal growth.

When the Sun forms a square with Mars, there's a surge of dynamic energy that can lead to assertiveness and even conflict. This aspect encourages you to channel your energy constructively rather than impulsively. Be mindful of handling disputes with diplomacy and patience.

When the Moon flows into Pisces, your emotions become fluid and compassionate. It's when you're in touch with your intuitive and empathetic side. You may feel a stronger connection to the unseen realms and a desire to help and heal.

The Sun's square to Pluto brings intensity and transformation to the forefront of your life. This aspect can lead to power struggles and a need to confront deep-seated issues. It's a time for shedding old layers and embracing profound change, but it may come with resistance.

Venus's conjunction with Saturn adds a sense of commitment and responsibility to your relationships. You're looking for lasting connections and are willing to put in the work to make them endure. This aspect encourages loyalty and a desire for stable partnerships.

Mars opposed Pluto begins as a cosmic showdown between the warrior and the underworld. This aspect can trigger power struggles and confrontations. It's essential to channel this energy into constructive endeavors and avoid unnecessary conflicts.

When the Moon moves into Taurus, your emotions become grounded and focused on comfort and security. This planetary ingress is when you appreciate life's simple pleasures and may find solace in nature or indulge in sensory experiences.

The New Moon marks a fresh start and a time for setting new intentions. It's a cosmic blank canvas for your dreams and goals. Use this lunar phase to plant the seeds of what you want to manifest in your life.

As the Moon enters Gemini, your emotions become more communicative and curious. It's a time when you seek intellectual stimulation and enjoy engaging in conversations with others. This lunar phase encourages learning and social interaction.

Venus's ingress into Aries adds a touch of spontaneity and passion to your relationships. You're more direct, assertive in matters of the heart, and drawn to exciting and fast-paced connections. This Venus transit encourages you to take the initiative in love and pursue what you desire.

MAY WEEK ONE

☾ As the Moon softly enters Cancer, your emotions take on a nurturing and intuitive quality. During this lunar phase, you might find yourself more connected to your home and loved ones.

☽ The conjunction of Venus and Neptune creates an otherworldly aura in matters of love and creativity. It's as if you're under a romantic and artistic spell. Your relationships become infused with compassion, empathy, and idealism. This aspect encourages you to explore the dreamy and enchanting elements of love and creative expression.

🦁 When the Moon transitions into Leo, your emotions become vibrant and expressive. It's a cosmic invitation to shine, seek recognition, and enjoy life to the fullest. During this lunar phase, your creative side flourishes, and you're drawn to activities that allow you to express your individuality.

🔄 Pluto's retrograde period marks a time of profound inner transformation. It's as if the cosmos is guiding you to revisit the depths of your psyche, uncovering hidden motivations, and facilitating personal growth.

MAY WEEK ONE

The sextile between Mercury and Jupiter amplifies your mental capacities and communication skills. It's a harmonious cosmic conversation that encourages expansive thinking and optimistic dialogue. This aspect supports learning, sharing ideas, and planning for the future.

As the Moon moves into Virgo, your emotions take on a practical and analytical tone. It's when you find satisfaction in taking care of details, organizing, and striving for perfection. This lunar phase encourages productivity and a desire to serve others.

Venus sextile Pluto adds depth and intensity to your relationships and creative pursuits. This cosmic connection invites you to explore love and art's profound, transformative aspects. You may find yourself drawn to passionate and soul-stirring relationships and artistic expressions that carry a powerful emotional impact. It's a time for uncovering hidden desires and experiencing the magnetic pull of attraction. You are encouraged to explore the depths of your emotions, nurture your relationships, and infuse your creative endeavors with enchantment.

As the Moon gracefully enters Libra, the cosmic spotlight shines on balance, harmony, and relationships. Your emotions seek equilibrium, and you're inclined to weigh options carefully. This lunar phase encourages you to appreciate beauty, seek diplomatic solutions, and foster connections built on fairness and equality.

Mercury's ingress into Taurus grounds your thoughts and communication in practicality and sensuality. Your words become deliberate and connected to the physical world. This period favors discussions about material matters, financial planning, and enjoying the pleasures of the senses. Your mind is steady, and you approach decisions with a deliberate pace.

When the Moon journeys into Scorpio, your emotions dive into the deep waters of transformation and intensity. It's a time of emotional regeneration, where you're unafraid to explore the shadowy corners of your psyche. This lunar transit encourages you to seek truth, embrace change, and forge powerful emotional connections.

MAY WEEK TWO

The Full Moon marks a culmination and a time for release. It's a moment of heightened emotions and awareness, illuminating areas of your life that require attention. This lunar phase encourages reflection, closure, and the celebration of your achievements. It's an excellent time for letting go of what no longer serves you.

Mercury's square with Pluto sets the stage for profound and transformative conversations. Your thoughts delve into the depths of truth and power but can intensify debates and power struggles. This aspect encourages you to dive into research and uncover hidden knowledge, but remember to use this insight wisely.

As the Moon shifts into Sagittarius, your emotions take on an adventurous and open-minded spirit. You crave exploration and intellectual expansion. This lunar phase encourages you to seek new horizons, engage in philosophical discussions, and embrace the freedom to express your beliefs. It's a time of optimism and a thirst for knowledge.

When the Moon moves into Capricorn, your emotions become grounded and focused on your ambitions and responsibilities. It's when you're more inclined to work diligently toward your goals. This lunar phase encourages discipline, self-control, and a sense of duty.

The conjunction of the Sun and Uranus is like a burst of innovative and electrifying energy. It sparks change, unexpected events, and a desire for personal freedom. This aspect encourages you to embrace your uniqueness, break free from routine, and explore new horizons with enthusiasm and a pioneering spirit.

Mercury's square with Mars intensifies your mental processes and communication style. It can lead to sharp, direct, and sometimes contentious exchanges. While it fuels your determination and decisiveness, it is essential to channel this energy constructively and avoid hasty or impulsive decisions.

As the Moon enters Aquarius, your emotions take on an independent and forward-thinking vibe. You desire to make a positive impact on the world. This lunar phase encourages open-mindedness and community.

MAY WEEK THREE

The Sun's sextile with Saturn brings stability and a sense of accomplishment to your endeavors. It's as if the cosmos offers a helping hand to solidify your plans and make progress. This aspect encourages responsible and practical actions, making it an ideal time for long-term projects and commitments.

As the Moon shifts into Pisces, your emotions become sensitive and intuitive. You're more in touch with your dreams, creativity, and the subtle undercurrents of life. This lunar phase encourages compassion, spiritual exploration, and a deeper connection to your inner world.

The Sun's transition into Gemini marks a time of curiosity, adaptability, and communication. You become more versatile and eager to learn, exchange ideas, and connect with others. It's a period that favors mental agility, making it an excellent time for intellectual pursuits and social interactions. This solar influence encourages adaptability and exchanging ideas in your interactions with others.

💜 Venus's trine with Mars is a harmonious dance of passion and desire. Your relationships and creative endeavors are fueled with balanced and vibrant energy. It's a time when you can express your affections and pursue your desires gracefully and assertively.

🌙 The Sun's sextile with Neptune bathes your life in a dreamy and imaginative light. This aspect encourages you to explore your artistic and spiritual side. You may find solace in creative projects, meditation, or acts of kindness. Your intuition is heightened, making it easier to connect with the mystical.

✳ The Sun's trine with Pluto is a powerful alignment that brings transformation and regeneration. It's like a cosmic rebirth, allowing you to let go of the old and embrace the new. This aspect encourages personal growth, empowerment, and a deep understanding of your strengths.

🪐 Mercury's conjunction with Uranus sparks innovative and unpredictable thinking. Your mind is open to fresh ideas and unique solutions. This aspect encourages you to embrace your individuality.

MAY WEEK FOUR

As Mercury enters curious Gemini, your mind becomes agile and inquisitive. You find joy in engaging in lively conversations and seek mental stimulation.

Mercury's sextile with Saturn brings practical and disciplined thinking. This aspect helps you plan and organize effectively, making it a good time for serious discussions and structured decision-making.

The New Moon marks a fresh beginning and an opportunity to set new intentions. It's like a cosmic reset button, allowing you to plant the seeds of your desires and initiate new projects. This lunar phase encourages introspection and the formulation of new goals.

Mercury's trine with Pluto intensifies your mental processes and communication. You're drawn to deep and transformative conversations, seeking to uncover hidden truths and make profound discoveries.

The Sun's conjunction with Mercury brings clarity and heightened mental acuity. Your thoughts align with your core self, making it easier to confidently and authenticate your ideas and intentions.

When the Moon gracefully moves into Virgo, your emotions take on a practical and analytical tone. You may find yourself paying more attention to detail, seeking order, and striving for perfection. This lunar phase encourages acts of service, health-conscious choices, and a focus on daily routines.

As the Moon glides into Libra, your emotions seek harmony, balance, and connection. You're drawn to creating peaceful and cooperative environments and may find yourself more diplomatic in your interactions. This lunar phase encourages relationships, art, and the appreciation of beauty. It enables you to find common ground and create a sense of beauty and peace in your interactions.

Venus sextile Jupiter is a delightful aspect that brings a sense of abundance and enjoyment. Your life is touched by good fortune and positivity. This aspect encourages social gatherings, indulging in the finer things, and expanding your affections. Your love life and social interactions are filled with joy and optimism, and you may experience fortunate opportunities or expansion in areas related to love and finances.

JUNE WEEK ONE

Mercury sextile Mars sparks lively and dynamic conversations. You're ready to express your thoughts and ideas with enthusiasm and assertiveness. This aspect encourages effective communication, making it an excellent time for negotiations and discussions.

Venus's ingress into Taurus introduces a sensual and earthy energy into your relationships and pleasures. You seek comfort and stability in your connections, valuing loyalty and sensual experiences. This transit encourages you to savor life's delights and cultivate a deeper appreciation for the finer aspects of existence.

When the Moon enters Scorpio, your emotions take on an intense and reflective quality. You're more attuned to the mysteries of life and may explore deep psychological insights. This lunar phase encourages transformation and a desire to uncover hidden truths. You may find yourself delving into more profound emotional experiences and seeking to discover greater wisdom. This lunar phase encourages introspection and a desire to embrace life's mysteries and complexities.

Mercury's conjunction with Jupiter opens the doors to expansive thinking and intellectual growth. Your mind is brimming with possibilities, and you're eager to explore new horizons. This aspect encourages optimism, learning, and the sharing of grand ideas with others.

Mercury's ingress into Cancer brings a more emotional and nurturing tone to your communication. Your words become infused with empathy and sensitivity, making it easier to connect with others on a deeper emotional level. This transit encourages heartfelt conversations and an increased focus on family and home matters.

Mercury's square with Saturn adds a touch of practicality and caution to your thinking. While you may encounter challenges in communication, this aspect also provides the discipline needed to tackle complex tasks and make long-term plans.

As the Moon moves into Sagittarius, you're drawn to new experiences and a broader perspective on life. This lunar phase encourages a sense of freedom, optimism, and a desire for personal growth.

JUNE WEEK TWO

⚖ Venus square Pluto brings intensity to your relationships and desires. You may confront power struggles and deep emotional transformations during this aspect. It's essential to navigate these energies with care and a willingness to face and heal underlying issues.

🌀 Jupiter's ingress into Cancer marks a significant shift in the cosmic landscape. Your focus turns toward emotional growth, nurturing, and family matters. Jupiter's influence encourages expansion in the realm of home and personal connections, offering opportunities for greater understanding and support.

🌚 The Full Moon is a culmination of energy and emotions. It's a time to celebrate your achievements and release what no longer serves you. This lunar phase encourages you to acknowledge your progress and consider the following steps on your journey.

💜 Mercury's sextile with Venus enhances your social and communication skills. You're more charming, diplomatic, and capable of expressing your affections. This aspect encourages harmonious interactions and creative exchanges with others.

⚡ Mars square Uranus creates an atmosphere of unpredictability and impulsive energy. It's like a cosmic lightning bolt that urges you to break free from constraints and seek independence. While this aspect can fuel innovation and daring actions, it also requires caution and mindfulness.

Jupiter square Saturn forms a challenging aspect that balances expansion with restriction. It's like a cosmic test of your plans and ambitions. This aspect encourages you to find a middle ground between growth and practicality, helping you develop a solid foundation for your long-term goals.

As the Moon moves into Pisces, your emotions take on a dreamy and compassionate quality. This lunar phase encourages empathy and intuition.

Mars's ingress into Virgo brings a more organized and detail-oriented approach to your actions and desires. You'll find satisfaction in taking care of tasks with precision and efficiency. This transit encourages you to be of service and make improvements in your daily routines.

JUNE WEEK THREE

⬧ As the Moon enters Aries, your emotions become more assertive and passionate. You'll feel a strong desire to take the lead, initiate new projects, and embrace challenges. This lunar phase encourages you to follow your instincts and assert your individuality.

▨ Jupiter square Neptune presents a complex interplay of faith and illusion. It's like a cosmic dance between your dreams and reality. This aspect encourages you to be cautious with your optimism and idealism, as it's essential to distinguish between genuine opportunities and wishful thinking.

☺ The Sun's ingress into Cancer marks the June Solstice, ushering in a new season. It's a time of emotional depth, home, and family. Cancer encourages you to nurture your connections and find a sense of security and belonging in your personal life.

🌍 The June Solstice is a pivotal moment when the Northern Hemisphere experiences the longest day and the Southern Hemisphere its shortest. It symbolizes a balance of light and dark, and it's a time to celebrate the changing of seasons, offering reflection and renewal.

The Sun's square with Neptune creates a haze of confusion and ambiguity. It's like a cosmic fog, making it challenging to see things clearly. This aspect encourages caution in making significant decisions and a need for discernment in understanding your dreams and intuitions.

When the Sun forms a conjunction with Jupiter, it's a time of expanded opportunities and optimism. It's like a cosmic blessing that enhances your confidence and brings a sense of abundance and growth. This aspect encourages you to embrace new possibilities.

The New Moon marks the beginning of a new lunar cycle, symbolizing fresh starts and intentions. It's like a cosmic blank canvas where you can set new goals and aspirations. This lunar phase encourages introspection and the planting of seeds for future growth.

Mercury's sextile with Uranus brings a touch of mental brilliance and innovation. It's like a cosmic spark that ignites your creativity and ability to think outside the box. This aspect encourages original ideas and exciting conversations.

JUNE WEEK FOUR

⬤ The Sun's sextile with Mars adds a dose of energy and motivation to your actions. It's like a cosmic battery charge, boosting your vitality and drive. This aspect encourages you to take assertive and confident steps toward your goals.

🐻 As Mercury moves into Leo, your communication style becomes more expressive and dramatic. You'll enjoy sharing your thoughts and ideas with flair and creativity. This transit encourages bold self-expression and a desire to be the center of attention.

⌛ Mercury's trine with Saturn fosters a disciplined and structured approach to your thinking and communication. It's like a cosmic teacher guiding you in organizing your thoughts with precision. This aspect encourages planning, practicality, and attention to detail.

🪨 Mercury's trine with Neptune adds a touch of inspiration and intuition to your communication. It's like a cosmic channel to the realms of imagination and dreams. This aspect encourages artistic and empathetic exchanges.

⚡ Venus conjunct Uranus is a powerful cosmic alignment that sparks excitement and a sense of unpredictability in your relationships and pleasures. It's like a heavenly bolt of electricity that jolts your heart and desires. This aspect encourages you to embrace spontaneity and explore unconventional forms of love and enjoyment.

Venus's ingress into Gemini brings a light and playful energy to your relationships and aesthetics. It's like a cosmic swirl of social charm and curiosity. This transit encourages variety and adaptability in your love life and creative expression, making it an ideal time for exploring different connections and interests.

Neptune turning retrograde signifies a shift in your relationship with the mystical and spiritual realms. It's like a cosmic call to revisit your dreams and ideals, diving deeper into your inner ocean of intuition and imagination. This retrograde period encourages self-reflection and a more profound connection to your spiritual path.

Venus sextile Saturn forms a harmonious aspect that blends love and responsibility. It's like a cosmic promise of lasting and meaningful connections. This aspect encourages you to create stability and structure in your relationships and creative pursuits.

Venus sextile Neptune is a celestial dance of inspiration and compassion. It's like a cosmic painting of love and artistry. This aspect encourages a deeper connection with your romantic and artistic visions.

Uranus's ingress into Gemini heralds a period of intellectual exploration and innovation. It's like a cosmic awakening of your mind to new ideas and possibilities. This transit encourages curiosity, versatility, and a willingness to experiment with novel concepts and technologies.

Venus trine Pluto forms a harmonious aspect that deepens your emotional and transformative connections. It's like a cosmic key to profound love and meaningful change. This aspect encourages powerful, passionate, and even regenerative experiences in your relationships and creative endeavors.

With the Moon's ingress into Capricorn, a sense of responsibility and ambition takes center stage in your emotional landscape. It's as if a cosmic mentor has arrived, encouraging you to approach your feelings with a structured and disciplined mindset. During this time, you may find yourself more focused on your goals and obligations, seeking to achieve a sense of order and accomplishment in your life.

The Full Moon, with its radiant glow, marks a pivotal moment in your emotional journey. It's like a celestial spotlight shining on your achievements, desires, and lingering emotions. This phase serves as a cosmic mirror, inviting you to reflect on your progress, celebrate your successes, and release what no longer serves you. It's a time for closure and the culmination of energy.

As the Moon transitions into Aquarius, a spirit of independence and innovation infuses your emotional experiences. It's akin to a cosmic maverick awakening within you, urging you to explore unconventional avenues in your vibrant life. During this phase, you may feel drawn to unique and progressive ideas, as well as nurturing your social connections.

Saturn's retrograde journey signifies a period of introspection regarding your responsibilities and long-term aspirations. It's as if a wise cosmic teacher has asked you to review the blueprints of your life. You are prompted to ensure that your ambitions align with your authentic desires and values. This introspective phase encourages you to make any necessary adjustments to create a solid foundation for your future.

With the Moon's entry into Pisces, your emotions take on a dreamy and empathetic quality. It's as if a cosmic artist has dipped their brush in the colors of the imagination and painted your emotional landscape with vivid, ethereal hues. During this phase, you may find yourself drawn to introspection, seeking a deep connection with your inner world, and fostering compassion for others. It's a time to explore your dreams, nurture your intuition, and connect with the mystical realms within you.

This week, the celestial transitions provide you with a diverse array of emotional experiences. Embrace this cosmic guidance to gain deeper insights into your emotions and personal growth journey.

The Moon's entry into Aries sets your emotional world ablaze with a burst of dynamic energy. It's akin to a cosmic starting gun, igniting your internal fire and inspiring a sense of adventurous spirit. During this lunar phase, you'll find yourself drawn to take the lead, charge ahead, and pursue desires with unwavering passion.

Mercury turning retrograde initiates a profound cosmic review in the realms of communication, thought, and self-reflection. It's as if the universe hands you a magnifying glass to closely examine your ideas, words, and how you connect with others. During this introspective phase, you're encouraged to revisit past conversations and situations, unravel any misunderstandings, and refine your thought processes. Mercury retrograde offers a unique opportunity to dive into the archives of your mind and explore unresolved matters, ultimately leading to growth and clarity.

As the Moon gracefully transitions into Taurus, a sense of stability and groundedness permeates your emotional landscape. This lunar shift acts like a cosmic anchor, allowing you to find comfort in the world.

JULY WEEK THREE

❤️ The harmonious aspect of Mercury's sextile Venus creates a celestial connection that aligns your mind and heart in perfect harmony. It's as if your thoughts and feelings engage in a graceful waltz, fostering sweet and meaningful communication. This cosmic alignment encourages you to express your emotions with tenderness and sincerity. Whether you're involved in heartfelt conversations or expressing your affection to loved ones, the energy of Mercury's sextile Venus infuses your interactions with warmth and grace.

With the Moon's transition into Gemini, your emotions take on an air of curiosity and communication. It's as if a cosmic storyteller awakens within you, urging you to share your thoughts and feelings with enthusiasm. This lunar phase enhances your intellectual curiosity, sparking a desire to engage in stimulating conversations and connect with others through the exchange of ideas. Your emotional world becomes a vibrant tapestry of thoughts, words, and connections with those around you, which offers unique opportunities for self-discovery, personal growth, and connection with the world around you.

☺ The Sun's ingress into Leo marks the beginning of a vibrant and expressive period. Leo, a fire sign ruled by the Sun, encourages you to shine and embrace your individuality. It's like the cosmic spotlight is on you, urging you to let your unique qualities and creativity flourish. During this time, you'll feel more confident and courageous, ready to take center stage in your life and pursue your passions with enthusiasm.

⚡ When the Sun forms a harmonious sextile with Uranus, it's as if the universe injects a dash of electrifying excitement into your world. Uranus is the planet of innovation and change, and this aspect encourages you to explore new horizons and break free from routines. Expect surprises and unconventional opportunities that can inspire personal growth and open doors to fresh experiences.

💔 Venus square Mars creates a celestial dynamic that might spark romantic tensions or conflicts within relationships. Venus represents love and harmony, while Mars symbolizes desire and assertiveness. When these two clash, it can feel like a cosmic tug of war between what you want and what your partner desires.

JULY WEEK FOUR

● A New Moon is a cosmic reset button, signaling a fresh start and the perfect time to set new intentions and goals. As the Moon and the Sun align in the same sign, you'll have the opportunity to plant the seeds of your desires and watch them grow in the coming weeks. It's an ideal time for self-reflection and setting intentions that align with your heart's most authentic desires.

● Sun opposed Pluto, which initiates a powerful and transformative period. Pluto represents deep, subconscious forces and regeneration, and this aspect can bring about intense changes and confrontations. It's like a cosmic revelation urging you to face hidden truths and release what no longer serves you. While this may be challenging, it ultimately paves the way for personal growth and profound transformation.

☾ Venus' ingress into Cancer brings a nurturing and affectionate energy to your relationships and creative expressions. Cancer is ruled by the Moon, emphasizing emotional depth and sensitivity. During this phase, you'll seek comfort and security in your connections with loved ones.

💔 When Venus forms a square aspect with Saturn, it's as if the cosmic stage is set for a challenging performance in the realm of love and relationships. This aspect introduces a complex interplay between the desire for affection and the weight of responsibility. You might feel like you're treading the delicate tightrope of the emotional connection while carrying the burdens of duty. It's essential to find a harmonious balance between your need for love and the practical demands of life. While it may introduce obstacles in your relationships, it also offers opportunities for growth and maturity. Take this time to strengthen your commitments and make them more enduring.

🌙 Venus's square to Neptune introduces a dreamy and enigmatic atmosphere to your love life. It's like navigating the misty waters of romance and emotions, where illusions and fantasies may cloud your judgment. This aspect can lead to misunderstandings or the tendency to idealize someone, creating a gap between your expectations and reality. During this time, it's crucial to listen to your intuition and employ a discerning eye when it comes to matters of the heart.

AUGUST WEEK ONE

With the Moon's transition into Sagittarius, your emotional landscape takes on an adventurous and open-hearted quality. It's akin to your heart yearning for new horizons and a broader perspective. This lunar placement invites you to explore life's diverse tapestry, seek out opportunities for personal growth, and embrace the spirit of adventure. You may find emotional fulfillment in learning and experiencing new things.

As the Moon shifts into Capricorn, a more pragmatic and duty-bound emotional energy settles in. It's as if a cosmic call to action emphasizes your responsibilities, ambitions, and long-term goals. During this lunar phase, you're likely to feel a sense of accomplishment when you tackle tasks and make progress in your professional life. Your emotions are aligned with your need for structure and achievement.

Mars's entry into Libra brings a sense of equilibrium and diplomacy to your actions. This cosmic shift encourages you to approach conflicts with a feeling of grace and cooperation, prioritizing the greater good over personal desires. Your efforts to maintain balance in your relationships are well-supported by this influence.

When Mars forms a trine with Uranus, it's as if the cosmic engines of innovation and bold action have ignited. This aspect encourages you to break free from the ordinary and embark on an exciting journey of self-discovery. Mars, the planet of action and desire, aligns harmoniously with Uranus, the planet of innovation and change. You'll find the courage to pursue your unique passions and explore new horizons with fearlessness.

However, Mars's opposition to Saturn casts a shadow of responsibility and discipline. It's like the cosmic taskmaster Saturn has set up a roadblock in the path of your ambitions. This aspect challenges your desires and demands that you navigate the hurdles with patience and perseverance. While it may feel like a frustrating obstacle, it's also an opportunity to build a solid foundation for your goals.

The Full Moon illuminates the sky, marking a powerful climax in the lunar cycle. Emotions are heightened, and the results of your efforts come to fruition. It's a time of culmination and revelation as the Sun opposes the Moon. Reflect on what you've initiated during this lunar cycle and make adjustments.

✎ Mars's trine with Pluto brings a surge of transformative energy. The dynamic synergy of Mars and Pluto empowers you to delve deep into your desires and harness your inner strength for growth and success.

🔄 With Mercury turning direct, the cosmic signal goes from "pause" to "play." Delays and miscommunications begin to clear up, allowing for smoother exchanges of information and progress in your plans. It's an ideal time to move forward with projects.

Saturn's sextile to Uranus creates a harmonious alliance between tradition and innovation. This aspect bridges the gap between structure and change. It encourages you to find ways to meet your goals while still respecting the wisdom of the past. It's a time to strike a balance between stability and transformation.

✎ Venus's conjunction with Jupiter is like a cosmic blessing for love and abundance. These two benevolent planets come together to expand your heart and your sense of prosperity. It's a time when your social and romantic life flourishes, and opportunities for joy and connection abound.

✦ The harmonious sextile between Mercury and Mars creates a powerful synergy like two cosmic allies teaming up to supercharge your mental and communicative abilities. During this celestial collaboration, your thoughts become laser-focused, and your words gain a newfound assertiveness. It's as if you're armed with a mental sword and a shield of confidence, making it an excellent time to tackle tasks that demand both intellectual agility and a proactive approach. Whether you're problem-solving, planning, or engaged in a spirited conversation, you'll find that your words cut through the noise with precision and purpose.

☽ While the Moon gracefully glides through the realms of inquisitive Gemini, the atmosphere is charged with curiosity and a thirst for knowledge. You become like a sponge, eager to absorb new information and ideas from your surroundings. This lunar influence provides the perfect backdrop for engaging in thought-provoking discussions, diving into books or courses, and reveling in the kaleidoscope of knowledge that surrounds you. Your mind is agile, flexible, and open to diverse perspectives.

AUGUST WEEK THREE

The encore of Mercury's sextile to Mars amplifies your mental acuity and assertiveness, providing you with a double dose of communicative prowess. This aspect gifts you with a keen ability to express your thoughts and ideas with unwavering conviction. It's as if your problem-solving skills are on steroids, and you can effortlessly cut the fog, arriving at solutions with ease.

As the Moon enters nurturing Cancer, the cosmic spotlight shifts to matters of the heart and home. Your emotional landscape becomes more tender and empathetic, encouraging you to deepen connections with loved ones and create an atmosphere of warmth and care. It's an ideal time for cozying up at home, preparing comfort food, and reveling in the intimate bonds of family.

When the Moon enters flamboyant Leo, your inner performer takes center stage. The cosmic energy encourages self-expression, creativity, and perhaps even a touch of dramatic flair. During this lunar influence, you feel inspired to share your unique talents with the world and bask in the spotlight. It's a time to infuse joy into your endeavors and let your creativity shine.

☺ As the Sun gracefully enters Virgo, you'll find yourself embracing a more practical, organized, and detail-oriented approach to life. Virgo's energy encourages you to pay attention to the finer points and take a structured approach to your goals and tasks.

🌑 The New Moon marks the start of a new lunar cycle, offering a fresh slate for setting intentions and embarking on new beginnings. It's a cosmic reset button, providing an opportunity to leave behind what no longer serves you and welcome in the energy of renewal.

⚡ When the Sun forms a challenging square aspect with Uranus, expect a burst of unexpected and revolutionary energy. This aspect can bring surprises, disruptions, and a desire for change. While it may be unsettling, it's also an opportunity to break free from routines and embrace innovation. Flexibility is vital during this time.

💜 Venus graces Leo with its presence, igniting a love for glamour, creativity, and self-expression. You'll be drawn to the spotlight, desiring appreciation and affection. Your artistic side shines, making this an excellent time for enjoying the arts or indulging in romance.

AUGUST WEEK FOUR

Venus's trine to Saturn brings stability and commitment to your relationships and creative pursuits. This aspect encourages lasting and meaningful connections. It's like a cosmic promise of long-term harmony and mutual support in matters of the heart and artistic endeavors.

Venus's sextile to Uranus adds an exciting, unpredictable element to your love life and social interactions. You'll be open to trying new experiences and meeting unconventional people. This aspect encourages spontaneity and infuses your relationships with a touch of excitement.

Venus's trine to Neptune deepens your emotional connections and artistic inspirations. It's like a celestial invitation to explore the depths of your feelings and express them through creative pursuits.

The harmonious sextile between Uranus and Neptune invites you to bridge the gap between the old and the new, the traditional and the visionary. It's a time when innovative and spiritual insights can coexist, fostering a sense of hope and renewal.

Saturn's entry into Pisces is a significant celestial event that prompts a reflective, soul-searching period. During this transition, your emotions and intuition will take center stage. You might find yourself more in tune with your inner world, experiencing a deeper understanding of your feelings and a heightened sense of empathy. It's a time to rekindle your connection with your dreams and aspirations, allowing your imagination to guide you toward a more profound purpose.

Mercury's journey into Virgo brings a heightened sense of detail-oriented thinking. Your cognitive skills receive a boost, making this an ideal time for structured, systematic tasks. Your organizational abilities shine, and you'll thrive in endeavors requiring precision. Focusing on health and well-being, both mental and physical, becomes a key theme.

As Mercury squares Uranus, expect a surge of mental energy and potentially surprising insights. This aspect fuels innovative thinking but can also make your mind a touch restless. Embrace new ideas and be open to cognitive flexibility, as this is a period to break free from habitual thought patterns and embrace change.

SEPTEMBER WEEK ONE

♈ The Mars Jupiter square ignites a fiery desire for expansion and adventure. You'll be brimming with the energy to pursue your goals and ambitions, but it's essential to maintain a sense of balance. Overextending yourself is a risk, so remember to pace your efforts. When managed wisely, this energy can lead to significant accomplishments.

🜨 With Uranus turning retrograde, you're encouraged to embark on a journey of self-discovery and internal exploration. This phase calls for a review of the changes and innovations you've experienced recently. Take time to integrate these new insights and find deeper meaning in your life. The key to personal liberation lies in understanding your unique path.

☺ The Full Moon is a time of culmination and realization. It's the moment to harvest the fruits of your intentions and goals set during the previous New Moon. Emotions may run high, so use this phase for self-awareness and introspection. It's a period of emotional reckoning and acknowledging your achievements. Seize this opportunity for self-discovery that the cosmos offers, and navigate with grace and wisdom. 🌠🌑

The Moon's shift into Aries heralds a dynamic and assertive emotional phase. You'll feel a surge of enthusiasm and a strong desire to take the lead in various aspects of your life. It's a time for initiating new projects, embracing your inner warrior, and tackling challenges with unwavering determination.

As the Moon moves into Taurus, a sense of stability and practicality permeates your emotional landscape. During this phase, you'll prioritize comfort and security, finding solace in life's sensual pleasures. It's an excellent period for tending to financial matters, seeking out beauty in your surroundings, and grounding yourself in the material world.

The harmonious Sun sextile Jupiter aspect showers you with optimism and opportunities. It's as if the universe is offering you a golden ticket to expansion and growth. This planetary shift is the perfect time to set ambitious goals, explore new horizons, and step outside your comfort zone with confidence. The world is your oyster, and you're ready to seize it.

When the Moon transitions into curious Gemini, your sociable and inquisitive side takes the spotlight. It is a phase brimming with intellectual curiosity and a strong desire to connect with others. Engaging in lively conversations, learning new things, and broadening your mental horizons will be highly fulfilling.

Mercury's sextile with Jupiter amplifies your communication skills and intellectual prowess. It's as if your words and ideas flow effortlessly, and your mental faculties are at their peak. It is an excellent period for making plans, embarking on educational pursuits, and sharing your thoughts with a broader audience. Your optimism and positive mindset shine through in your interactions.

The Sun's conjunction with Mercury brings your thoughts and self-expression into perfect harmony. During this alignment, your intellect is sharp, and your communication is clear and impactful. It's an auspicious time for crucial conversations, making important decisions, and articulating your ideas with precision. Your ability to express yourself and connect with others is at its zenith.

The delightful alignment of Venus sextile Mars infuses your romantic life with a harmonious rhythm. Love and desire sway gracefully together, creating an atmosphere of passion and connection. This celestial dance encourages a more profound understanding between partners, promoting unity and cooperation in both existing and budding relationships.

However, Mercury's opposition to the stern taskmaster Saturn can pose challenges to effective communication. This aspect may lead to difficulties in expressing your thoughts and feelings clearly, often resulting in severe or critical conversations. Patience and a thoughtful approach are crucial to overcoming these verbal hurdles.

As Mercury strides into diplomatic Libra, a shift towards balanced and harmonious communication prevails. Your discussions take on a more cooperative tone, making it an ideal time to resolve conflicts and promote mutual understanding. Diplomacy and fairness become your guiding principles.

SEPTEMBER WEEK THREE

✿ Venus' entrance into pragmatic Virgo encourages a more analytical and systematic approach to your romantic endeavors. You may find satisfaction in paying attention to the finer details of your relationships, helping to maintain their health and functionality.

⚡ The square between Venus and Uranus introduces an element of unpredictability into your love life. Sudden changes or unconventional romantic interests might arise. These surprises can add an exciting and dynamic dimension to your relationships.

☻ However, the Sun's opposition with responsible Saturn may present challenges in terms of self-expression and personal authority. You might encounter obstacles that require patience, determination, and a mature outlook to overcome. This aspect encourages growth through facing difficulties head-on.

● The arrival of a New Moon symbolizes new beginnings. It's the perfect moment to set fresh intentions and embark on a journey of self-discovery and personal growth. This lunar phase invites you to plant the seeds of your aspirations.

Mars, the fiery planet of action and desire, has stepped into Scorpio. This celestial move ignites your life with a renewed sense of purpose and intensity. It's as though your inner passions are now on display for the world to see. Your desires are profound, and you're more willing to go to great lengths to pursue your goals. This cosmic alignment empowers you to tackle challenges head-on and to transform your dreams into reality.

The September Equinox marks a significant transition as the seasons shift. It's a pivotal moment in the year, urging you to find equilibrium in your life. Just as nature adapts to changing seasons, you, too, must adjust to life's ever-evolving circumstances. This period invites reflection and realignment with your goals and priorities. It's a time to let go of what no longer serves you and embrace the fresh opportunities that lie ahead.

However, the Sun's opposition with Neptune introduces an element of illusion or confusion. While your intentions are noble, there's a risk of idealizing situations or individuals. This aspect reminds you to maintain clarity and discernment. Seek practical solutions to challenges that arise.

✦ The Sun's trines with Uranus and Pluto bring a potent blend of transformation and innovation into your life. These aspects encourage you to embrace change and open yourself to new ideas and experiences. You'll find that you're more adaptable and resilient during this period, making it a fertile ground for personal growth.

☽ As the Moon moves into Scorpio, your emotional depths are stirred. It's a time for delving into your innermost feelings and motivations. This lunar phase encourages introspection, self-discovery, and understanding of the deeper drives behind your actions.

🔋 However, the square between Mars and Pluto can intensify power struggles and conflicts. It's essential to approach such situations with tact and diplomatic touch. Avoid provoking confrontations and instead seek common ground or compromise where possible.

🏔 The Moon's subsequent entry into Sagittarius brings a sense of adventure and expansion. Your emotions take on a more open and exploratory quality. It's as if the universe is encouraging you to broaden your horizons.

When the Moon gracefully glides into Aquarius, it's as if a refreshing cosmic breeze sweeps through your life. This airy sign infuses your emotions with a sense of freedom and individuality. You may find yourself drawn to innovative ideas, social causes, and intellectual exploration. It's a perfect time to connect with like-minded individuals who share your visionary outlook and to contribute to group efforts that aim to make the world a better place.

However, be mindful of a Mercury square Jupiter aspect that's in play. While your enthusiasm and optimism are running high, there might be a tendency to be a tad overly optimistic. You could get caught up in the grand vision of things and overlook crucial details.

As the Moon gently drifts into Pisces, your emotional landscape takes on a dreamy, ethereal quality. You might find yourself more compassionate and empathetic toward others, making it an ideal time for acts of kindness and acts of service. It's also a period when your creative and spiritual sides can flourish. Dive into artistic projects, meditation, or lose yourself in music or literature.

A shift occurs as the Moon enters Aries, infus. with a burst of dynamism and courage. You're eag pursue your personal goals and dreams wi enthusiasm. Your assertiveness and fearlessness take the spotlight, motivating you to charge forward.

Meanwhile, Mercury's entry into Scorpio brings depth and intensity to your thought processes. You're inclined to delve beneath the surface and investigate matters thoroughly. Secrets and hidden truths may hold a particular fascination for you during this time. Your communication becomes more probing, making you an astute observer and conversationalist.

With the radiant Full Moon gracing the skies, it's a period of illumination and culmination. It is when you see the results of your efforts and intentions set during the New Moon phase. It's a moment of clarity, reflection, and realization. Take this time to release what no longer serves you and step into the light of your achievements.

However, a square between Mercury and Pluto injects a dose of intensity into your communication and thought processes.

s the Moon gracefully strolls into Taurus, envision serene landscape where your senses come alive. This celestial placement encourages you to ground yourself, finding joy in the simple pleasures that the physical world offers. Allow the comforting energies of Taurus to guide you, fostering a deeper connection with the material realm and a heightened appreciation for the beauty that surrounds you.

The harmonious sextile between Venus and Jupiter is akin to a cosmic blessing, infusing your connections with warmth and generosity. Your social circles expand, and an air of grace prevails in your interactions. It's a time to savor the richness of life and share these moments of abundance with those who hold a special place in your heart.

As the Moon transitions into chatty Gemini, your mind becomes a playground of ideas. Intellectual curiosity takes the spotlight, urging you to engage in lively conversations and explore new realms of thought. Let the free flow of ideas stimulate your mental faculties, creating an atmosphere ripe for learning and expression.

OCTOBER WEEK TWO

Venus, now gracing Libra, engages in a celestial dance with stern Saturn. This interplay introduces a touch of tension into matters of love and aesthetics. Striking a balance between your desires and practical considerations becomes pivotal during this cosmic choreography. Embrace patience and diplomacy as you navigate through these nuanced dynamics.

Venus, now donning the charm of Libra, encounters an opposition with dreamy Neptune. This cosmic rendezvous introduces an air of enchantment but also a potential for ambiguity. Be mindful of idealizing situations or relationships, and strive for clarity in matters of the heart.

Pluto's direct motion serves as a cosmic catalyst, initiating a profound transformation. It's as if the universe is encouraging you to release the remnants of the past and embrace the evolution that awaits. This period beckons inner growth and a courageous shedding of what no longer aligns with your higher purpose.

Venus, engaging in a harmonious trine with the innovative Uranus, injects excitement into your love life.

As the Moon gracefully enters Virgo, a cosmic spotlight illuminates the details of your daily life and routines. This lunar phase invites you to find satisfaction in the minor, intricate aspects of your existence. Take a moment to appreciate the precision and order in your surroundings, allowing a sense of purpose to guide your actions.

The Sun's square with Jupiter introduces a celestial conversation between self-assurance and expansive optimism. While confidence propels you forward, be mindful not to let overconfidence tip the scales. Finding a harmonious balance between ambition and realism will be your cosmic challenge during this celestial alignment.

Transitioning into Libra, the Moon ushers in an air of harmony and social grace. Your cosmic task involves seeking equilibrium in your relationships and interactions. Embrace diplomacy, cooperation, and the pursuit of beauty, aiming to create a balanced and aesthetically pleasing environment.

NOVEMBER WEEK TWO

⟳ Mercury, the cosmic messenger, embarks on its retrograde journey, initiating a period of introspection and review. This phase prompts us to revisit old projects, relationships, and unresolved issues. As communication may experience delays and misunderstandings, it's a time to exercise caution and practice patience. Mercury's retrograde is an invitation to delve into the past, reassess our trajectory, and ensure that your path aligns with your intentions.

🐱 The lunar spotlight then shifts to Leo, infusing the cosmic stage with creativity and self-expression. This phase encourages each of us to tap into our inner performer, engaging in activities that bring joy and radiating our authentic light into the world. It's a celestial call to embrace the bold and vibrant aspects of your personality, allowing your creative spirit to shine.

🔍 Amidst this cosmic tapestry, Jupiter, the planet of expansion, takes a reflective pause as it turns retrograde. The retrograde period becomes a heavenly retreat, allowing us to delve into our inner landscapes, refine our aspirations, and recalibrate our journey toward personal and spiritual evolution.

NOVEMBER WEEK THREE

As the radiant Sun forms a harmonious trine with expansive Jupiter, the cosmic energies align to bring a sense of optimism, growth, and good fortune into your life. It's a time when your confidence and enthusiasm are boosted, encouraging you to reach for new heights and explore opportunities with a positive mindset.

The Sun's trine with stabilizing Saturn further enhances this period, grounding your aspirations and providing a solid foundation for your endeavors. Practicality combines with optimism, allowing you to make long-lasting and meaningful progress in various areas of your life.

Mercury, the planet of communication and intellect, engages in a transformative dance with powerful Pluto through a sextile. Your thoughts become more profound, and your ability to uncover hidden truths is heightened. This cosmic alignment encourages deep introspection and insightful conversations.

Shifting into Scorpio, Mercury dives into the depths of emotions and mysteries. Your mind becomes attuned to subtle nuances.